CHINA
the land

Bobbie Kalman

The Lands, Peoples, and Cultures Series

Crabtree Publishing Company

The Lands, Peoples, and Cultures Series
Created by Bobbie Kalman

Writing team
Bobbie Kalman
Christine Arthurs

Editor-in-Chief
Bobbie Kalman

Editors
Janine Schaub
Christine Arthurs
Margaret Hoogeveen

Research
Moira Daly
Virginia Neale
Alison Tharen

Design and layout
Heather Delfino
Margaret Hoogeveen

Printer
Worzalla Publishing Company
Stevens Point, Wisconsin

Illustrations
John Mantha p. 9
Mitchell Beazley p. 13

Photography acknowledgments
Cover shot: Ken Ginn
Jim Bryant: p. 10(top and bottom), 11(top), 16, 19, 20, 21(center); Ken Ginn: p. 4-5, 21(bottom), 23(right),
26(full page); Pat Morrow/First Light: p. 6, 11(bottom right), 18; Gayle McDougall: Title page, p. 8, 9(left),
25(center), 26(inset), 31; Courtesy of the Consulate General of the People's Republic of China: p. 7,
11(bottom left); Courtesy of the Royal Ontario Museum: p. 12, 15; Peter Reid: p. 17(top and bottom right), 27;
Larry Rossignol: p. 25(top left), 28(both); Caroline Walker: p. 9(right), 14, 17(bottom left), 21(top), 22, 30(inset);
Xian Visual Arts Company: p. 29; Xu Jiayan: p. 25(bottom), 30(full page); Zhao Meichang: p. 25(top right).

Contents

The land of China

Over the centuries countless travelers have journeyed to China and marveled at its ageless treasures. In recent decades, however, China was closed to tourists, and very few outsiders were allowed to enter its borders. In the 1980s China was opened once again. Hundreds of thousands of visitors rushed to discover this great country.

Superlative!

How should we begin to talk about such a vast country? When people describe the many wonders of China, they often use superlatives. Superlatives are words such as highest, biggest, most, hottest, and longest. Let's find out why people from all over the world find the land of China to be such a fascinating place.

A fascinating country

China has the **most** people in the world. One quarter of the world's population, over a billion people, make China their home. China is the third **biggest** country, next to the U.S.S.R. and Canada. Its history dates back four thousand years. This makes China the **oldest** civilized country. Where is one of the world's **hottest** deserts? You guessed it! It is in China, and it is called the Taklimakan Desert. The world's **highest** mountains are the Himalayas, found on the border between China and Nepal. The **tallest** of these is Mount Everest. The Chinese Grand Canal is the **longest** canal in the world. The **largest** structure ever erected is the Great Wall of China. It winds through almost six thousand kilometers of valleys and mountains. The Great Wall is the only structure made by human beings that can be seen from the moon!

A land of many variations

Travel across China, and you will be amazed at the variety of landscapes and range in climates. Take hiking boots and sandals, a warm coat, a bathing suit, an umbrella, and a water bottle. You will need them all!

Step by step

You can explore China's geography in three huge steps. The top step is the west of China. It includes enormous mountains and the largest plateau in the world, the Plateau of Tibet. A plateau is a flat, elevated area of land. Tibet is known as "the roof of the world" because its average height above sea level is four thousand meters. Most of the countryside is covered with patchy shrub and grasslike vegetation. Tibet is a cold place! Its frost-free period is less than fifty days a year.

Look way up!

Mountains cover over one third of China's enormous land mass. The Himalayan Mountains are on the border of Tibet and Nepal. Mount Everest, the world's highest peak, is part of this range. This mountain, called *Qomolangma* by the Chinese, is 8848 meters high and still grows about a centimeter every two years as it continues to form!

Going down

On the second step are smaller mountain ranges and huge deserts. The Qilian Shan, the Qin Ling, and the Kunlun Mountains are on this middle level. Two of China's main river systems, the Yellow and the Yangtze, originate in the heights of the Kunlun Mountains.

High and dry

To the northwest the great mountain ranges enclose desert basins. One of these is the Taklimakan Desert. It is so hot in this region that raindrops evaporate before they touch the ground. Sandstorms last for days, and huge, shifting dunes seem to come to life as the wind shapes them.

(opposite) Mountain climbers attempt to scale China's Mount Everest, the world's highest peak.

The Gobi Desert is one of the world's biggest deserts. A large part of it is in the Mongolian area of northern China. Extreme temperatures are found within the vast area of the Gobi Desert. The temperature soars to 45°C in some areas and, because of the northern location and high altitude, the temperature can also drop below -40°C. Instead of sand, the Gobi desert is mostly made up of rock and gravel.

Planting trees keeps the desert sands from overtaking the surrounding farmland.

Coastal plains

On the last and lowest step are the coastal plains. These plains are just above sea level and extend along the coast of the South and East China seas. This land is very fertile, and the weather is warm and wet. Ninety percent of China's people live in these areas.

China's rivers

The two major rivers in China are the Yellow and the Yangtze rivers. The Yellow River system is one of the world's major water highways. At 5590 kilometers in length, the Yangtze is the fourth-longest river in the world. Its Chinese name, *Chang Jiang*, means "Great River." Both the Yangtze and the Yellow rivers flow from the high western mountains to the lower eastern regions.

Flood waters: friend or foe?

Rivers are a source of life. Their waters provide riverside communities with fish, and their silt fertilizes the areas of land close to the water. For centuries the great rivers of China flooded the countryside around them. These flood waters left behind rich soil carried down from the higher lands. Over time these areas have become huge, flat, fertile basins. The Yellow River basin, for example, is the most important flat land in China's northeast. The soil in this area is formed from fine, windblown yellow-gray dust from the Gobi Desert. The land is fertile and holds moisture well. It is ideal for agriculture.

As well as being a source of life, rivers can also be a source of disaster. The Chinese call the Yellow River "China's Sorrow." In the past three thousand years it has overflowed more than 1500 times, causing much damage and costing many lives. To control floods, the Chinese have built high banks of earth, called dikes, along the edges of their rivers.

Yu the Great

The first dike builder in ancient times was a skilled engineer named Yu. Over four thousand years ago Yu and countless helpers worked thirteen years building dikes to prevent the overflow of the Yellow River. His project was a success, and Yu was made emperor. According to Chinese legend, the Yellow River did not flood again for over a thousand years, and Yu became known as Yu the Great.

Swimmers enjoy a refreshing dip in the Li River beside the picturesque Guilin hills.

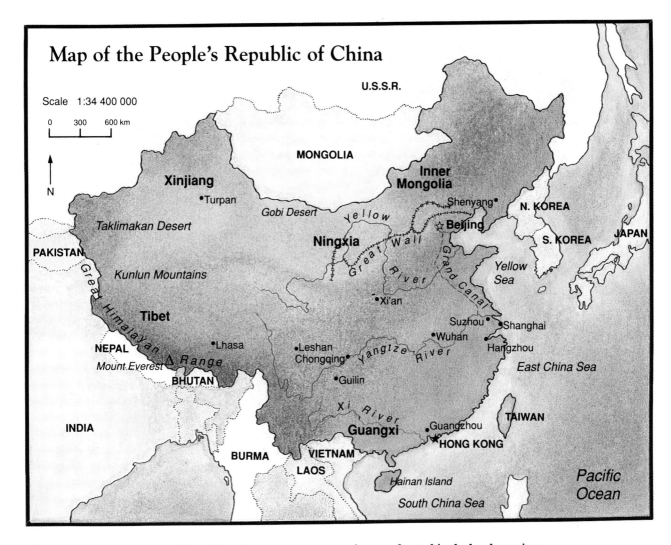

Map of the People's Republic of China

Scale 1:34 400 000

0   300   600 km

N

U.S.S.R.

MONGOLIA

Xinjiang

•Turpan

Gobi Desert

Taklimakan Desert

PAKISTAN

Kunlun Mountains

Great Himalayan Range

Tibet

•Lhasa

NEPAL

Mount Everest

BHUTAN

INDIA

BURMA

Inner Mongolia

Shenyang•

N. KOREA

☆ Beijing

S. KOREA

JAPAN

Ningxia

Yellow River

Great Wall

Grand Canal

Yellow Sea

•Xi'an

Suzhou• •Shanghai

•Wuhan

Hangzhou

•Leshan
Chongqing•   Yangtze River

East China Sea

•Guilin

Xi River

Guangxi   •Guangzhou

TAIWAN

★ HONG KONG

VIETNAM

LAOS

Hainan Island

South China Sea

Pacific Ocean

Eleven countries border on China. China's five autonomous regions are located in the border regions.

River water is diverted to irrigate rice paddies and create fish farms where fish such as carp are raised.

People in Yichang Park watch the busy river traffic along the Yangtze River.

The faces of China

Now that you have explored the landscapes of China, it is time to meet the people who live in this enormous country. The population of China consists of fifty-six nationalities. Most of the people are Han Chinese. These people, who make up ninety-four percent of the population, can trace their ancestors back to the time of the Han Dynasty, which ruled China from about 206 B.C. to 220 A.D. The Han share a distinct Chinese culture although they speak different dialects of the same language.

A multicultural country

The fifty-five other cultural groups in China total around sixty million people. They are called "minorities" because, all together, they make up only six percent of China's huge population. The appearance, clothing, and languages of the minority peoples differ dramatically from group to group. This variety in customs and traditions makes China an exciting multicultural country.

Autonomous regions

Most of the Han Chinese live in the eastern part of China. The majority of the non-Han groups live in the west and northwest. These vast, lonely pasturelands are called "autonomous regions." The five autonomous regions of China are Xinjiang, Inner Mongolia, Guangxi, Tibet, and Ningxia. They are governed by China, but their inhabitants are allowed to follow some of their own traditions and customs.

(circle) This food vendor is a member of the Han nationality, who make up 94% of the population.

(inset, opposite) A young Tibetan wears a kerchief to protect herself from the harsh plateau winds.

(opposite, bottom) After their tai ji quan exercises, four elderly Han Chinese gather for an early morning chat in a Hangzhou park.

(bottom left) Two young girls from Suzhou wear their traditional regional costumes as they make slippers.

(bottom right) Uygur children dressed in colorful clothing live in the autonomous region of Xinjiang.

China's first emperor, Qin Shi Huang Di

People have lived in China for hundreds of thousands of years. The bones of a few of the earliest people on earth have been found there. One of these is Lantian Man, who lived 600 000 years ago; another is Peking Man, who lived around 350 000 years ago.

An ancient civilization

China's civilization, which is more than four thousand years old, was ruled by emperors. The Chinese believed that the emperor's right to rule came from heaven. In fact, the Chinese word for emperor means "Son of Heaven." When an emperor died, his title was passed on to a member of his family, usually his eldest son. The son then became the next ruler. A series of rulers from the same family was called a dynasty. The word dynasty also refers to the period of time during which one of these families ruled. During its long history China has been ruled by several dynasties.

Some famous dynasties

Here are a number of important events and cultural contributions from the reigns of several Chinese dynasties:

Zhou (1100-476 B.C.) Confucius and Lao Zi, two great Chinese thinkers, lived and wrote. The first canals were built.

Qin (pronounced Chin) (221-206 B.C.) China took its name from this dynasty. The Great Wall was built.

Han (206 B.C.-220 A.D.) The majority of China's people trace their ancestry back to this dynasty. Paper was invented and acupuncture was first used. Buddhism came to China from India.

Sui (589-618) The Grand Canal was built.

Yuan (1279-1368) The Mongolian Kublai Khan conquered and ruled. Marco Polo visited China.

Ming (1368-1644) The works of Ming architects, artists, and philosophers earned China the reputation of being the most civilized country in the world. The Forbidden City was built.

Qing (pronounced Ching) (1644-1911) China saw many changes, including the introduction of the locomotive. The last emperor, Pu Yi, belonged to the Qing dynasty.

Keeping to itself

During most of its ancient history, China had little to do with the rest of the world. Its rulers felt that the Chinese could not learn anything from other cultures because their own achievements were already far superior. Chinese leaders also feared that outside contact might lead to invasions by foreign powers. They were right to have this fear!

The travels of Marco Polo

Although China was not interested in the rest of the world, the world was interested in China. Stories told by a famous traveler named Marco Polo intrigued the people of Europe. In the thirteenth century Marco Polo and some fellow adventurers traveled by land from Venice, Italy to Cambaluc, China. To travel such a great distance by land was virtually unheard of in those early days. Marco Polo and his caravan crossed Europe and Asia and traveled along the Silk Road north of the Taklimakan Desert. He became friends with Kublai Khan, the Mongolian ruler of China, and stayed in China for seventeen years before returning home with colorful silks and beautiful porcelains.

Trading with the outside world

By the sixteenth century many countries began to send out explorers and traders to China. Before long, Britain became China's major trading partner. Chinese silks, teas, and porcelain were sold for a great profit in England. To get these treasures, the British traders supplied China with opium. A great number of Chinese people became addicted to this dangerous drug. The Chinese fought several wars with the British to stop them from bringing opium into China.

Problems with foreigners

More and more foreign countries wanted control over China and its treasures. China was not strong enough to keep fighting the numerous wars that were waged against it. As a result, it lost many battles and was forced to open several of its ports for trade. One of these ports was Hong Kong, which was leased to Britain until 1997, when it will become part of China once again.

Marco Polo lived in China for seventeen years and later wrote a book about his adventures in this great country.

13

By the turn of the century there were so many foreigners in China, it appeared that China would be divided up into colonies belonging to several foreign countries. This angered the Chinese people very much.

Father of the country

Sun Yat-sen, a medical doctor, saw that the people of China were poor and unhappy. A small number of rich and powerful people owned all the land, and the peasants did all the work, receiving very little for their labors. Sun Yat-sen wanted to help the poor people, so he formed the *Kuomintang*, the Chinese Nationalist Party. He had many followers because he promised to rid China of all foreigners and turn over the land to the peasants. In 1912 the nationalists forced the Qing emperor, Pu Yi, to give up the throne. China became a democratic republic, and Sun Yat-sen was made president. He is still greatly respected as a national hero because he got rid of the emperor and the foreign powers. The Chinese call him *kuo-fu*, meaning "father of the country."

The Communist Revolution

Unfortunately, Sun Yat-sen was not able to unite the hundreds of millions of poor people, and his government could not solve China's many problems. Military commanders, called warlords, seized control of the country. In 1921 the Chinese Communist Party was created, led by a dedicated man named Mao Zedong. For almost thirty years the communist and republican parties fought against each other for control of the government. Finally, on October 1, 1949 the fighting ended, and Mao announced the formation of the People's Republic of China, a communist state.

Mao Zedong

The people of China trusted Mao Zedong, and his communist government was finally able to unify China. Mao set up farming communes and sent all the children to school. While he was leader, hardly any foreigners were allowed into China. The Chinese worked towards making China a modern industrial country. Mao's great desire was to see China become a strong, independent nation.

Mao Zedong

Unfortunately, Mao's plans for modernizing China were not very successful. Instead of offering rewards for hard work, Mao wanted people to make many sacrifices. He felt that they should work for the good of China and not for their own private gain. During Mao's time there was little growth in industry or farm production. Nevertheless, for many years the Chinese respected Mao Zedong as the wisest man in China. His picture appeared everywhere, and everyone carried little red books filled with Mao's words of wisdom.

Deng Xiaoping

Shortly after Mao Zedong died in 1976, Deng Xiaoping came to power. He realized that, although Mao helped unify China, he had also made some serious mistakes. Deng saw that China was far from its goal of being a modern industrial country. To solve this problem, he encouraged people to work harder. His government allowed people to earn extra money by selling crops grown on their private land. Within five years production in China doubled. After many years of being shut off from the rest of the world, China once again began allowing foreigners and new ideas to cross its borders.

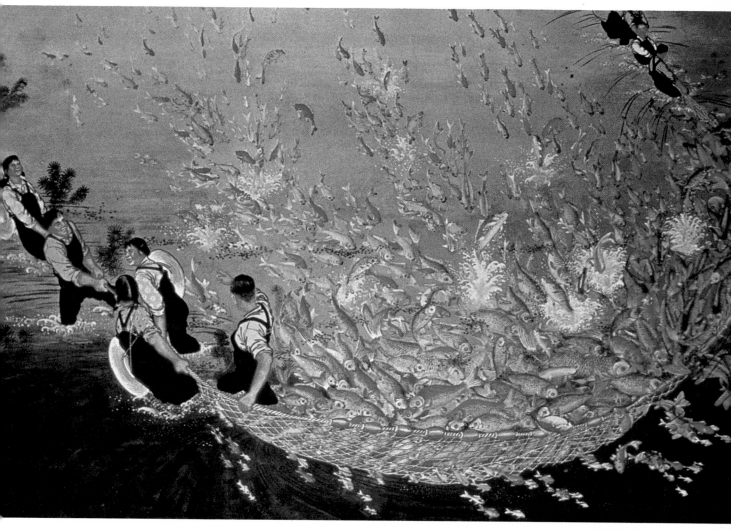

This Chinese painting illustrates how communism should work. Fishermen are shown pooling their efforts so their whole village can share the catch.

Ideally, through cooperation and communal endeavor, more work could be accomplished, and people should reap greater benefits. In practice this system rarely works.

What is communism?

Since 1949 China has been a communist country. Communists believe that all resources should be owned by the whole society. Land, food, and the goods produced by the people are owned in common. The government decides what crops are grown on the land, what products are manufactured in factories, and what prices should be charged for both. It also assigns people's jobs and the location of their workplaces. Under communism, the government plays a big role in the lives of its people and allows them little say in the way they are governed.

The democracy movement

The people of China are not satisfied with their system of government. In June of 1989 thousands of students staged a protest in Tienanmen Square. They wanted the right to elect their government. They wanted their newspaper and television stations to have the freedom to report the truth instead of what the government ordered them to report. These requests were answered by gunfire. Hundreds were killed and many were thrown in prison. Some students were executed in the days that followed. The Chinese people were defeated in Tienanmen Square, but their hope for democracy lives on.

China has experienced many changes in the last ten years. During that time the government has been using a different system to run the country. As a result, industries are producing more goods, and new products are being developed. China is becoming a modern, industrialized nation.

An open policy

After years of remaining closed to foreigners, China adopted an "open policy." It is now eager to learn about new business methods. China has also begun encouraging other countries to invest money in Chinese businesses. The result of these investments is "joint ventures." Joint ventures are businesses that are owned jointly by Chinese and foreign investors.

The responsibility system

For many years China has tried to provide its people with food and jobs. With such a large population, however, the government was unable to look after everyone. Since the beginning of the 1980s China has encouraged people to make extra money on their own. This new way of making a living is called "the responsibility system." Instead of telling people what jobs they should have, the government wants individuals to be responsible for their own decisions and incomes. People are being encouraged to start private businesses.

An open-air free market

The newly rich

Each day newspapers report stories of private businesses that have opened up and are prospering. Many Chinese people are becoming quite wealthy and are able to own things that they could only dream about having in the old days. Motorcycles, automobiles, television sets, and flush toilets are just a few of the purchases of the newly rich.

Free markets

Farmers now grow extra crops on their private plots of land. These crops are sold at free markets, and the farmers are allowed to keep the money they make from their sales. Free markets are markets that are not controlled by the government. Those who are not farmers are able to make money in other ways. They can provide services or sell goods that they have made. Barbers, dentists, pet-supply vendors, and outdoor cooks compete for customers at the open markets. Everyone is busy trying to make a living.

Bursting with business

As well as owning land, people are now allowed to own homes. There is more food, and workers are earning higher wages. Trade is booming. China is producing iron, cement, textiles, aircraft, television sets, and even satellites. By the mid 1980s China ranked fourth among the world's steel producers and seventh among oil producers.

Tourism, a new industry

At first the new tourist industry created many jobs and brought a lot of money into the country. People from all over the world wanted to discover the "new" China. Hotels popped up in every major city. The events in Tienanmen Square, however, have dampened the enthusiasm of many potential visitors. In the months following, the number of tourists fell drastically, and the new hotels stood mostly empty.

Bejing's Great Wall Sheraton is one of China's famous luxury hotels housing international tourists.

(right) Many imported goods are now available in China, as shown by this billboard advertisement.

A department store window in Shanghai displays the latest goods available for children.

Growing pains

China is experiencing a number of growing pains. Not everyone finds it easy to adjust to a new way of life. The responsibility system is good for hard workers and highly trained people. These people are finding it much less difficult to make extra money than the other members of the population. Farmers who do not live near big towns or cities have problems transporting their crops to the free markets far away. Some must walk for hours to reach a marketplace. Under the communist system prices were fixed by the government. Now the prices of food and other goods are rising rapidly. The cost of living is going up faster than the incomes of many people who are unable to do extra work or sell extra crops.

Coping with many changes

Being part of a new system in China means taking many risks. Many Chinese are finding that the responsibility system has left them without jobs. New employment practices have also begun to cause friction in the workplace. Those who have become managers now earn more money than their fellow workers. This practice upsets some people because, under the old system, everything was shared by the members of a work group. Some people think it is unfair that managers earn more money than other employees.

The sun sets through a haze caused by coal pollution in Beijing. China's cities are all experiencing pollution problems due to increased industry.

There is a lack of clean water in China's cities. This woman must wash her vegetables in a polluted river.

The widening gap

In the early days of communism the people of China were equally poor. Today some are getting very rich. The gap between the rich and poor is growing wider. When poor villagers see some of their neighbors getting richer and richer, problems are bound to arise. What might some of these be?

Pollution problems

The changes that have taken place in China have affected the lives of everyone. Some of these changes have produced serious problems. Due to the recent explosion of industry, factories are running overtime to produce as many goods as possible. Manufacturing so many products is good for China's economy but terribly harmful to the environment.

Dirty water, air, and land

China has not yet developed modern methods of dealing with its wastes. More than 85 000 factories are constantly dumping large quantities of waste into China's waters. One fifth of China's rivers are polluted, and one quarter of these are contaminated with dangerous substances.

Using coal is a major cause of air pollution. Most people in China still use coal for heating and cooking. Many industries also use coal as their primary source of energy. When coal is burned, it sends out a thick, black cloud of smoke. Breathing this smoke is a health risk.

Household garbage is simply dumped onto the land outside cities. Garbage dumps are contaminating both the land and the underground water supplies around them. As a result, people who live near rubbish sites are experiencing all sorts of health problems.

Few pollution controls

There are few pollution laws to stop China's factories from spewing harmful fumes into the air and dumping toxic chemicals onto the land and into its waters. As China races to become an industrial nation, it must deal with its serious environmental problems immediately, or the consequences will be tragic for its people and the rest of the world!

Food for a billion!

Half the working people in China are farmers. That's a lot of farmers for a country that has very little land suitable for farming. Much of China is too steep, too cold, or too dry to support crops.

Fertile plains and basins

Crops grown in China vary from region to region. The plains of northern China are covered with fertile topsoil. This soil, formed from the yellow-gray dust of the Gobi Desert, is rich in lime and holds moisture well. Wheat is the main crop grown on these flat, northern fields. The land also yields good crops of beans, potatoes, cabbages, tomatoes, melons, onions, corn, and millet. Besides these crops, China grows forty-three percent of the world's cotton. It produces more cotton than any other country!

The southeast is China's most productive agricultural region. The fertile Yangtze and Xi river basins are here, and the weather is so mild that crops grow all year round. In a single year a farmer can produce two crops of rice and a third crop of barley or winter wheat. Nearly one half of China's total rice crop is grown in this region. That is why this area is called "China's rice bowl." Peanuts, lichees, citrus fruits, sweet peas, sugar cane, and tea are grown in the southeast.

Farming every bit of land

In order to feed such a large population, the Chinese need to farm every bit of land. They plant one type of crop between the rows of another so they will be able to produce as many crops as possible. They even grow food on the sides of roads and railway lines. Some farms are located in the middle of the cities. City farms grow mostly fruit and vegetables, but poultry, pigs, and dairy cows are also raised there.

Terraced fields are cut into hillsides to make more land available for farming rice and vegetables.

(opposite, top) The water buffalo is a valuable work animal.

Hands-on labor

Farm life is hard work in China. Most of the farming is done without the use of modern machinery. Tractors are only used on half the farms in the country. Plowing is usually done with wooden plows pulled by water buffalo or oxen. Simple tools such as sickles, hoes, and harrows aid the farmers with their manual labor. The farmers work very hard and put in long days!

Rice farming

Spring is the beginning of the rice-growing season. First, rice seeds are planted in a nursery. While the seeds are sprouting, farmers prepare the rice fields, or paddies. Manure and nightsoil are mixed into the soil to make it more fertile. The farmers then build low walls of earth, called dikes, around the paddies so water cannot seep out. Next, the fields are flooded with water. Farmers use a harrow to mix the water with the sun-baked earth.

Plenty of care and water

Planting is usually done by hand. Farmers wade into paddies and place the delicate shoots into the ground one by one. These brilliant emerald-green beds of seedlings need constant care. Paddies must be weeded, and the water level checked regularly. As the plants grow, the water level is raised. When the stalks are golden yellow, the rice plants are fully grown and ready to be harvested.

Harvest time

At harvest time the farmers open the dikes and drain the water from the paddies. When the paddies have dried, the rice plants are cut down with sickles. The long stalks are collected, bundled, and laid out to dry. Once dry, the rice grains are removed by hitting the plant. This process is called threshing. The loose grains are collected in sacks and transported to factories where the shell around each grain is removed. Then the rice is packaged to be sold.

(center) A field worker labors in a wet rice paddy.

(bottom) Farmers ladle water onto a variety of vegetables that are grown together on an inner-city farm.

Fishing

Besides growing food on the land, the Chinese also harvest the waters for fish—an important food supply. Along the coastline people use nets to catch seafood such as mackerel, shrimp, shark, eel, grouper, squid, and crab. Huge nets are cast into the water and dragged along the seabed. One third of a catch is sold; the rest is divided among the crew.

Almost twice as many freshwater fish are caught in China as in any other country in the world. Using poles and nets in the traditional way, fishermen catch some freshwater fish in China's lakes and rivers. Three quarters of all the fish caught in China, however, are raised on fish farms. Fish farms are ponds in which fish such as carp are bred.

Fishermen often work into the evening. To see one balancing on his raft as the sun sets behind the hills of Guilin is one of the prettiest sights in China.

Fishing with cormorants

Cormorants are glossy, black birds that dive for fish. These birds are well known for their large appetites. They were used by fishermen in many areas of the world until new fishing methods using modern equipment made them unnecessary. The only place where cormorant fishing is still practiced is along the gentle rivers in the south of China. Fishermen in these regions use cormorants because the rocky river beds prevent them from using nets.

Diving for fish

Cormorant fishing requires only a few simple tools. These consist of a narrow wooden raft or large tub, a long bamboo pole, and several well-trained cormorants. The fishermen use their pole to steer their craft and guide the birds. They splash the water with the pole to encourage the birds to dive. Each bird dives deep and swims underwater until it catches a fish in its beak. Every bird has a leather collar fastened tightly around its neck to prevent it from swallowing the catch. After a cormorant comes back to the raft, the fish is pried from its beak. A dozen trips later its collar is loosened, and the bird is allowed to swallow one fish before going back to work. If the fisherman happens to lose count and tries to take the twelfth fish from the cormorant, the bird protests noisily. Not only do cormorants know how to count, they also know their wages!

The cities of China

China's cities are growing and changing very rapidly. Twenty of them have populations of over a million people. As time goes by more and more people are moving to the cities to work in factories. Streets, bicycle paths, markets, and waterways are always crowded. Let's visit some of China's cities and find out what makes each of them unique.

Beijing, the capital

Beijing is the capital of China. It used to be called Peking. Like many Chinese cities, Beijing is a mixture of old and new. Over the years it has expanded far beyond the old city walls. These walls were knocked down in the 1950s because their narrow double gates were slowing down traffic. Many factories have been built on the outskirts of Beijing since then. The manufacturing of machines, chemicals, agricultural equipment, and textiles are important industries in Beijing. Beijing has also become an important tourist area and receives thousands of visitors each year.

At the heart of the city is the Imperial Palace, also known as the Forbidden City. It was built by the Ming emperors in the early fifteenth century. The palace was called the "Forbidden City" because ordinary people were forbidden to go near its gates. Only government officials and members of the emperor's family were allowed to enter. Today the Forbidden City is open to the public. Its buildings have been converted into museums.

The great port of Shanghai

Shanghai, China's largest city, is China's major port. Can you guess what its name means? It means "on the water." Shanghai is China's leader in business and trade, and a wide variety of modern goods can be found there. Because Shanghai is a port city, it has many foreign visitors. Their influence can be seen everywhere. The people of Shanghai know more about western ways than the people in other Chinese cities.

The Venice of the East

The city of Suzhou is a beautiful city along the Grand Canal. Suzhou is called the Venice of the East because, like the city of Venice, it is criss-crossed by rivers and canals. People live and trade along the banks, and many families live on *sampans* right on the water. A *sampan* is a houseboat with a flat bottom. Suzhou is one of the oldest cities in the Yangtze basin. For centuries it has been famous for its charming gardens and beautiful silks.

City on the roof of the world

Lhasa, located 3660 meters above sea level, is the capital of Tibet. Its remote location, its fascinating mix of old and new, and its multicultural flavor make it an exciting city. Ancient monasteries are now being restored, and new luxury hotels are being built there. All kinds of people dressed in traditional costumes mingle with tourists from all over the world in the streets and open markets. Tibetans make pilgrimages to the Lama Buddhist temples. Kazaks, a group of nomads who live in western China, come to Lhasa to sell their meat and crafts.

The enchanted hills of Guilin

The city of Guilin is set deep in the mountains of the Guangxi autonomous region in the south of China. Guilin is surrounded by jagged limestone peaks and mist-covered valleys of rice fields. Over the centuries these hills have been sculpted by water and wind, producing bizarre shapes and eerie underground caves. The Chinese boast that "the best scenery under heaven is found near Guilin." As a result, Guilin has become a busy tourist center with many hotels and a growing population.

(opposite, top left) Many ancient Chinese scroll paintings feature scenes of the picturesque Guilin hills shown in the background.

(circle) In Suzhou many homes must be approached by boat through connecting canals.

(top right) Lhasa, the capital of Tibet

24

The Liberation Day parade arrives in Tienanmen Square, the largest public square in the world, located near the Forbidden City.

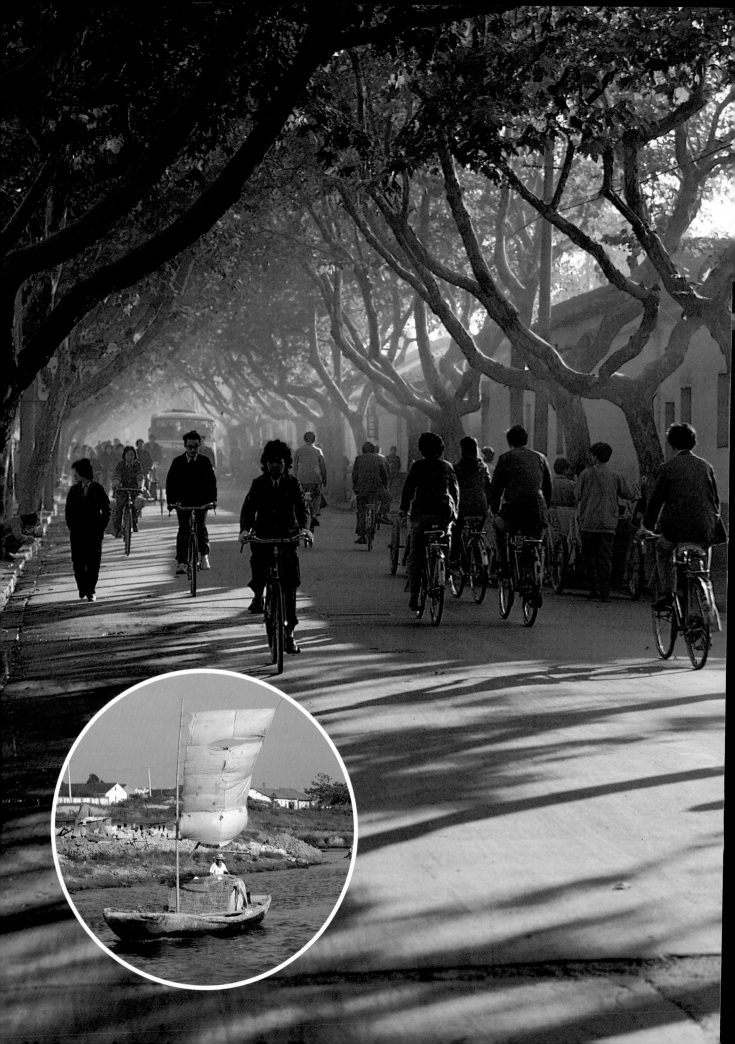

Getting around in China

People have found many ways to get from place to place in the huge country of China. Travel by water has traditionally been the easiest method of reaching distant locations. Over thousands of years the Chinese built a vast system of canals to improve the natural travel routes. The most famous of these, the Grand Canal, stretches 1790 kilometers from Beijing in the north to Hangzhou in the south. It links five rivers and winds through four provinces. China's many rivers and canals are still crowded with *junks, sampans*, and all kinds of other water vehicles. *Junks* are sailboats used for carrying cargo, and *sampans* are floating homes.

As well as water "highways," modern China has extensive train routes, paved roads, and more than two hundred air routes crossing the country. Highways and airways are commonly used to transport cargo, whereas trains remain the most popular mode for travelers.

A Chinese train ride

When people have to travel long distances, they usually travel by train. This is not surprising when you learn that there are about sixty thousand kilometers of train tracks criss-crossing China's huge area. Train cars are always overflowing with passengers and their possessions.

There are two ways to travel by train in China: hard class and soft class. The seats in hard class are wooden benches. In soft class, the seats are like couches and are much more comfortable. Soft-class seats are usually occupied by Chinese government officials and foreign travelers. In both hard class and soft class, passengers can look forward to being served hot water for tea.

Millions of bicycles

For local travel, bicycles are the most popular means of travel. There are more than two hundred million bicycles in China! Sometimes there are so many riders in the streets that they ride ten or twelve abreast! On wider roads special bike lanes are set up with dividers to separate bicycle and motor-vehicle traffic. The most treasured two-wheeled vehicle is the motorbike. So many people want to own motorbikes that their names must be put on long waiting lists.

New car owners

In the past, government officials were among the few people to own automobiles. Today other people are buying them, too. As with motorcycles, names are put on waiting lists. If many people buy automobiles, China will have some terrific traffic jams!

The buried soldiers of Xi'an

Did you know that there is a strange kind of buried treasure in China? Twenty-two centuries ago life-sized sculptures were buried in the tomb of the first emperor of the Qin dynasty, Qin Shi Huang Di. The sculptures remained undisturbed in this tomb until the twentieth century. When archeologists began to explore old ruins in the city of Xi'an, they discovered the amazing underground army, complete with more than seven thousand terra-cotta soldiers, real weapons, chariots, and bronze horses. Scientists have restored some of the sculptures that were damaged over time. Others have been left buried in the ground for future archeologists to uncover. Tourists from all over the world travel to Xi'an to see these lifelike soldiers!

The friendship bear

The giant panda has been named one of China's national treasures. No one is quite sure whether this cuddly looking creature belongs to the bear or the raccoon family, but people are certain that they want it to survive in its Chinese homeland. China has set up ten nature reserves for the panda. The most important one is the Wolong Nature Reserve, operated with the help of the World Wildlife Fund.

There are fewer than a thousand pandas left in the whole world! For more than half-a-million years they roamed the region north and south of the Yangtze River. Today much of their natural habitat has been destroyed. Many of the native bamboo forests where the pandas lived and found food have been chopped down to make room for new farmland and roads. Nature does not seem to favor the panda either. Every 40 to 120 years large areas of bamboo plants die off. When this happens, many pandas starve to death. The last bamboo die-off was in 1983.

(opposite) Thousands of tourists visit the stone forest to marvel at the incredible rock formations.

(inset, opposite) The panda could be nicknamed the friendship bear because many concerned people from countries all over the world have made lasting friendships while trying to save this rare animal.

One of the thousands of terra-cotta soldiers found buried in a tomb in Xi'an

The stone forest

The famous stone forest is located in Yunnan province. This is not a forest of trees. It is a large area of limestone pillars that seem to be growing out of the earth. These limestone formations were pushed up by the shifting earth hundreds of years ago. Powerful currents from underground rivers carved out caves and other fascinating forms in the rock. People climb to the tops of the incredible rock pillars to get a breathtaking view of the surrounding countryside.

The Grand Buddha

The city of Leshan in Sichuan province is the home of the Grand Buddha. This huge sculpture of a seated Buddha is seventy meters tall. Construction, which began in the year 713 A.D., took ninety years to complete. The Grand Buddha overlooks three rivers and was built to protect water travelers. Many boating accidents had occurred at the spot chosen for the statue. People hoped the Grand Buddha would watch over them and prevent any further accidents. (See pictures on following page.)

 # The Great Wall

Throughout history many civilizations have built walls to defend themselves against outsiders. By far the most famous of these is the Great Wall of China. Under the first emperor of China, Qin Shi Huang Di, work began on the Great Wall. It was not a totally new construction. Building it involved linking together and fixing many walls that already existed from earlier times. As a result, the wall curves and loops through the mountains like a snake.

Back-breaking work!

As you might expect, undertaking such a project was no easy task. Portions of the wall were built on steep mountainsides. Laborers had to struggle to find secure footing. They sweated and strained from dawn until dusk, carrying huge boulders right up to the summits. The boulders were used to construct two thick walls running alongside each other. Tons of earth, lugged in heavy baskets, were dumped in the space between the two barriers. The laborers then pounded the earth into a hard surface with heavy wooden mallets.

Maitraya, or Buddha of the future, is this statue's name.

Landmark earth

The Great Wall is the largest structure in the world. It curves across three provinces and stretches nearly 6400 kilometers from Beijing to the deserts of Inner Mongolia. The wall is built on a bed of wide, square stones. Along the way are towers that were used by soldiers watching out for possible attacks. The wall is so wide in some places that several horses can gallop along the top; it is so tall that a person would have to stand on the shoulders of two other people in order to see over it. It is so long and massive that it is the only structure made by human beings that can be seen from the moon!

A spectacular view

The Great Wall of China has become a world-famous tourist attraction. People from around the world and native Chinese alike are amazed by the wall that stretches as far as the eye can see. The view from the wall at dawn and sunset is absolutely spectacular! One day perhaps you will take a walk on the Great Wall or sit on the toes of the Grand Buddha!

31

Glossary

altitude - The height of land above sea level

ancestry - The family line from which a person is descended

autonomous - Free from outside control; independent

civilization - A society with a well-established culture that has existed for a long period of time

colony - An area taken and controlled by another country

commune - A community in which land is held in common, and where members live and work together

contaminate - To poison or pollute

culture - The customs, beliefs, and arts of a distinct group of people

democracy - A type of government in which people elect representatives to make decisions for society

dialect - A way of speaking that differs from the standard language in some of its vocabulary, pronunciation, and sayings

harrow - A horse-drawn farm tool, with a heavy frame and disks, used for breaking up ploughed land

investment - Property or another possession that will increase in value in the future

joint venture - A business owned in common by two persons, companies, or governments

junk - A flat-bottomed sailing ship

Kazaks - Tent-dwelling nomads living in the autonomous region of Xinjiang in western China

lichee - A small round fruit with a brittle red shell and juicy white flesh

limestone - A hard type of rock used for building

minority - A small group that differs from the larger group of which it is a part

monastery - A place where men live together as a religious community

multicultural - A term used to describe a society composed of a number of different cultural groups

national group - People who share a common background and lifestyle

nature reserve - A place where animals and plants can live undisturbed by people

nightsoil - Human waste used as fertilizer

nomads - People who travel from place to place in search of food or land on which to graze animals

pilgrimage - A religious journey to a sacred place

plain - A treeless area of land that is flat or nearly flat

plateau - An area of flat land that is higher than the surrounding land

sampan - A small boat with one sail and a flat bottom, often used as a houseboat

sea level - The average height of the surface of the sea

sickle - A curved hand tool that is used for cutting grass, grain, or weeds

silt - Fine sand or clay that is carried by water and deposited at the mouths of rivers

summit - The highest point

terra-cotta - Hard reddish-brown pottery

thresh - To separate grain from husks and straw

toxic - Poisonous

vendor - A person who sells goods

western - The term used to describe people from the western part of the world, especially Europe and North America, as opposed to people from Asia, such as the Chinese and Japanese

Index

89 WP Printed in the U.S.A. 876